THE GATE
SETHIAN GNOSTICISM IN THE POSTMODERN WORLD

ED. RUNE ØDEGAARD

Published 2012 by Krystiania

© Rune Ødegaard 2012

Cover: Rune Ødegaard and Joachim Svela

ISBN 978-82-998243-8-5

Contents

About this book 8
Acknowledgments 10
Preface 11
Introduction to The Book of Eleleth 15
The Book of Eleleth 17
    The vision in the Chapel 17
    The Origin 18
    The Mother 19
    The Son 20
    The Four Lights 21
    Man 22
    The Fall 23
    Yaldabout and Nebroel 25
    Metanoia 27
    The creation of Man 28
    Man and the Fullness 28
    Adam, Eve and the Serpent 30
    Cain, Abel and Seth 32
    The Seed of the Great Seth 34
    Yaldabout wants to destroy the Children of Seth 35
    Seth as Jesus 36
    Seth establishes the baptism through Jesus 37
    Seth's orders to his descendants 38
    The end of the vision 39
Introduction to The Book of the Guardian Angels 41
The Book of the Guardian Angels 43
    The Children of Seth 43
    The Sons of God are born 44
    The sons of Seth and the daughters of Cain 44
    The misguided souls of the earth are calling for Yaldabout 47

The great ship	48
The Children hide and the arrival of the flood	49
Yaldabout's covenant with the Children of earth	50
The Children of Seth receive Guardians	51
The work of redemption continues	51
Introduction to The Book of Horaia	53
The Book of Horaia	54
Horaia's self-presentation	54
The companion of Seth	55
Barbelo, the ever-being	56
Closing words	61
Introduction to The Book of Zorakatora	63
The Book of Zorakatora	64
Zorakatora comes into existence	64
Zorakatora's self-presentation	65
The work of Zorakatora	65
The blessing and the curse of the Priest-prophets	67
Zorazoraia comes to existence	68
The Great Commission	69
Introduction to The Traveler	71
The Traveler: The Names of Transformation	72
Introduction to The Book of Specularis	75
The Book of Specularis on The Kin and the Angel	76
Introduction to The Purple Tablet	79
The Purple Tablet	80
Introduction to The Hymn to the Mission of Aberamento	83
The Hymn to the Mission of Aberamento	84
Introduction to John and the Masks	87
John and the Masks	88
Introduction to The Book of Adamas	91

- The Book of Adamas 91
- Introduction to The Book of Time 115
- The Book of Time 116
  - The Vision in the Chapel.. 116
  - Seth speaks... 117
  - Cain and Abel.. 118
  - The vision of the wandering of the Children of Seth 120
  - The redemption of all?.. 121
  - The Commandments of Eleleth 122
  - Closing words.. 123
- Afterword... 124
- Appendix 125
  - A self presentation of Sodalitas Sanctum Seth................... 125

And the snake bade the woman to eat of the fruit, and said:
Eat and be wise.
And the woman ate and became wise, and she gave of it to her husband,
Who gave of it to his son,
Who gave of it to his children,
Who gave of it to their children,
And so they continued.
Today I turn to you, with these very same words:
Eat and be wise!

About this book

This book is a selection from the text collection *Charaxio*, the holy book of the organization *Sodalitas Sanctum Seth* (SSS). It is the SSS that has authorized my publication of these texts.

In the first book of this Sethian trilogy, the following was said concerning the Charaxio:

In the early Sethian texts, it is said that Seth hid his secrets on the top of a mountain. This mountain is referred to as mount Charaxio.

This is probably not a mountain with a physical location in the world, but another place in another dimension, a place in mind, dream, or wakeful sleep. The description of this central mountain has associated the Sethians with people living in the mountains.

The doctrine that was hidden on Charaxio is like a pattern of archetypal dream images, which might be compared to an archetypal 'radio station'. Sethians tap into this channel for inspiration.

In the Sodalitas Sanctum Seth the *Charaxio* is also a book. This book consists of three parts. The first part is the old Sethian texts, and consists currently of The Apocryphon of John, The Book of the Great Invisible Spirit, The Hypostasis of the Archons, The Thought of Norea, The Naassean Psalm, The Three Steles of Seth, Trimorphic Protenoia, The Apocalypse of Adam, Allogenes, The Book of Allogenes, Melchizedek, Marsanes, Zostramos, The Gospel of Thomas, and The Gospel of Judas. The Gospel of Thomas and The Naassean Psalm are not described as Sethian texts, since the Sethian mythology is not directly connected to these books. However, they are still used within the modern manifestation of the tradition.

The second section consists of explanations, interpretations, narratives, and letters. This part of the Charaxio is an expression of the vitality of the tradition. It requires that the Sethians are constantly able to express gnosis in an original way, as language creates the reality we all are part of.

The third part consists of rituals, ceremonies, instructions for practice, and Gnostic sacraments.

The Charaxio is not a canon, as a canon is a fixed form, congealed by history and culture. The Gnostic journey is individual and cannot be explained in simple dogma; Life itself is our canon. Rather, the Charaxio can rightly be called a book of inspiration, or a compass for the Gnostic journey.

The texts published here are selected to draw attention to important parts of the mythology of modern Sethianism. They are chosen because they provide a good outline of the tradition, and do not necessarily represent my own opinions. The Book of Eleleth was the first book to be published from the Charaxio, and was included in the first book of this Sethian trilogy, namely The Key: Sethian Gnosticism in the Postmodern World. It is also included in this book, as it is one of the most important texts of this tradition. It can here be seen in context with a more comprehensive collection of manuscripts.

This collection also shows the Sethian view on the development of history from the beginning via the Creation to the Flood, and introduces some important characters, such as Zorakatora, Zorazoraia and Aberamento.

There are many other texts that might have been relevant to include in this book, but I think that these texts will provide a good starting point for using the keys given in the first book of the trilogy. It is therefore my recommendation that you read The Key: Sethian Gnosticism in the Postmodern World before you study this book.

Acknowledgments

I want to thank everyone who has helped me with this book, and especially Dennis D, Lori, Ellen H and David J for proofreading. I am also grateful for all the positive feedback from readers of my first book, The Key: Sethian Gnosticism in the Postmodern World.

Last but not least, I want to thank Kjersti and Joachim, of the Krystiania project, for their invaluable support.

Preface

This is the second book in a trilogy on the Sethian Gnostic tradition as it is practiced today. The first book dealt with the key concepts in the tradition, to give the reader a key to reach beyond the written word in the texts.

This second book builds on the first one in the sense that the reader will only fully benefit from the contents of the present work if he or she was able to unfold the mystery of the last book. The previous book presented tools to the reader so that he or she could grasp the key of the Mystery with the hands of the soul, a key that is located at the bottom of the Well of Consciousness.

The intention of this book is not to continue that project, but to further cultivate the understanding that the reader may have acquired. Through this book, I intend to give new perspectives to those who in their wanderings have stumbled upon an encounter with Metanoia, Our Lady of Unexpected Insight and Perplexity, and thus perceived the shape of the Mystery through the veils of the mind.

With these crossroads of attainment as background, my readers have at least two very different approaches when reading the present book. They can either read it as a curious interpretation of the stories of the Bible and a collection of tales, or as refreshing wine for the existential Gnostic pilgrimage in the postmodern era.

The eye of the beholder is thus of crucial importance. In themselves, these stories are just fairytales; but if you take part in them, and project your life and experiences into them, they come to life and become the source of the important transformation of you becoming yourself. And thus you may uncover the truth that the Gnostic story is really the story of your life. Consider, therefore, this entire book as a projective test, like projective tests in the field of psychology. These tests have no meaning themselves; it is you, with your background, your opinions, your cultural frame of mind and your self-understanding that determin what you might find between these covers.

It is therefore difficult to find the right words to present these texts. Is it suitable to conjure up a courteous bow, or some similar friendly and inviting literary gesture? Probably not, for you are your own host in receiving these Sethian books.

As in the previous book, it is important to remember that when you are approaching writings of this nature as you read this book, the book is also reading you.

So drape yourself in the dark cloak of the pilgrims of our tradition, and pick up your rod of wandering, and step out to begin a Sethian journey.

Rune Ødegaard
Oslo, Norway
Winter Solstice 2011

The seal of Amarantus

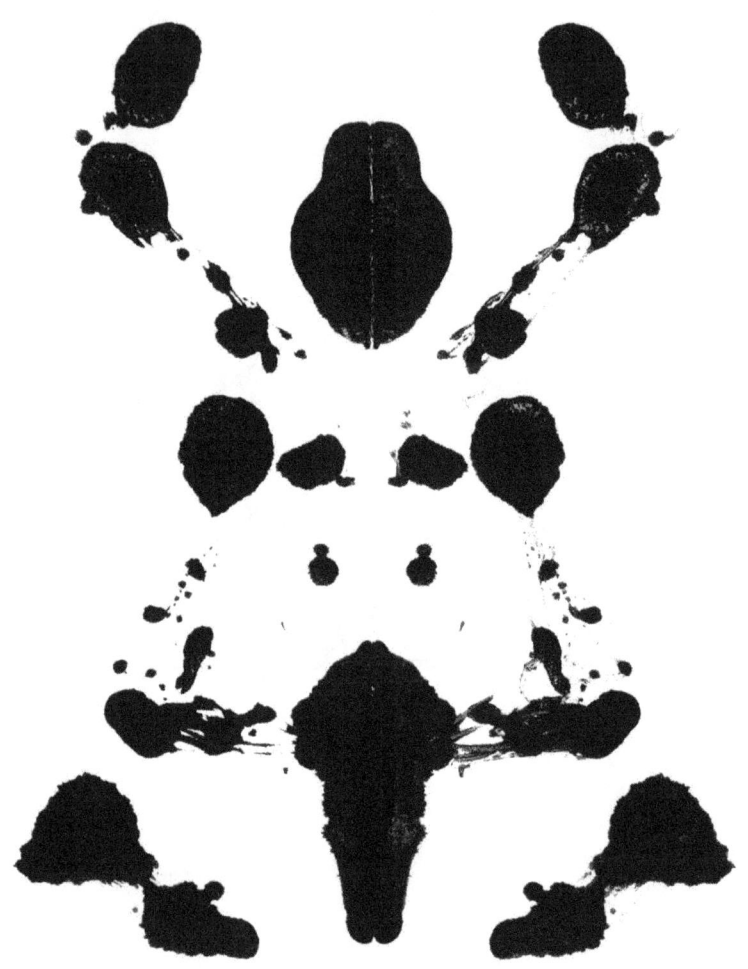

Introduction to
The Book of Eleleth

The book of Eleleth contains the Sethian teachings on the Creation and provides a new and unique perspective on the story that is described in Genesis. The book also presents events that predate the Creation described in the Bible. The Book of Eleleth is closely related to both The Secret Book of John and The Book of the Great Invisible Spirit (also called The Gospel of the Egyptians). Together these three books are facets of the same Sethian core doctrine and mythology.

The Book of Eleleth presents many of the central figures in Sethian mythology, and gives an indication of their qualities.

The frame of the story is Eleleth's visit to the Sethian Master in a chapel known as The Chapel of the Four Luminaries. The Four Luminaries to which the chapel is dedicated are Armozel, Oriael, Daveithai and Eleleth. The last of these entities appears as a mentor and initiator into the Sethian spiritual lineage on earth.

By reading the story of Master Amarantus' meeting with Eleleth, the Sethian relationship to angels and other spiritual beings are clarified. Angels are instructors and mediators. They are mediators in the same way that teachers are mediators. They are carriers of knowledge and understanding, which, through interaction with the human mind, open up our mental doors.

The order of the Aeons and the hierarchy of the Rulers are revealed to Amarantus. This revelation, which comes to him in the form of a vision, points toward the sacrament of the Ascension. In the Ascension, the individual participates in a visionary journey, performed with an initiator.

The sacrament of the Ascension follows the Baptism, which is also called The Baptism of the Five Seals. In the frame story Seth himself transmits these Seals to the narrator.

The frame story indicates how Amarantus was initiated into the Sethian mysteries. That is how the myth was revealed and how the sacraments were transferred. This is also how the Sethian tradition is reborn in this new era as 'Amarantian Sethianism'.

All the central keys and secrets of the tradition are hidden or partially obscured in this text. This story is the very foundation of the Sethian tradition of the Sodalitas Sanctum Seth.

The Book of Eleleth

The vision in the Chapel

Late one evening when I was lonely and alone in the Chapel of the Four Luminaries, the Holy Spirit came over me and covered me in a Golden Cloud. When I gave way to the perfect rapture, I heard a wonderful voice coming to me from all sides. I opened my soul's lips, and my heart asked the loneliness: Who are you? And the voice answered and said:
"I am true Light, Light that dissolves the darkness of the heavenly velvet night. I am the force that pulls the veil aside for those who live in the kingdom of the warring forces. I am the Light that glows, that warms or devours. I am what you might recognize and comprehend in the Abode of Darkness, but rise and see me with the eyes of the Man of Light, and you will see me as Eleleth, the guide from the Fullness in this abode, and you will realize that you are Seth and Christ, Father and Mother, the indivisible unity. As I am one with the Father, so are you one with me."
He reached to me with his hands. The left was as covered by bright peacock feathers, and the right as the dove's winter plumage.
He then said: "Be thou innocent as the dove and as cunning as the snake, and I will guide you, and the angel in you, on the paths of revelation."

He then said: "The light was moving. Darkness came to be. Search and you shall find, for the truth is wrapped in the very cradle of lies."
I felt an infinite urge for freedom, union, and love and the Infinite realm. And the Great Light said:

"The door is the broken heart and the key is the reconciled mind."
"I will teach you the truth about your origin and the creation of the Aeons, but only if you listen as a Living being are you able to hear my words, for the Light is for the Light and darkness for the darkness."

Suddenly, I was released from my abode and in the Light I experienced the beginning, even though my body never moved from the place I was seated.

THE ORIGIN

The origin of the Origin, is a perfect fulfilled and indivisible entity. He is not he nor she, as no such category can grasp Him. He is all qualities in perfect unity and harmony, nothing is missing, nothing needed, and nothing requested. He is the perfect rest in which He contemplates His nature in the great silence, in the Light surrounding Him of which is the source of the Living Light-Water.

He is a being, yet not a being as we usually perceive a being. He is boundless in His being for in Him is no limit, no centre and no extent. He is like an eternity in an eternity; it is He who is God and the origin of all. He is The Great Invisible Spirit which is above all that is, was, and ever shall be.
He has no part in the Aeons or in time. He does not exist in anything lower or higher than himself, since everything is in Him. But he is united with them all.
He has no name, as no one was before him to give a name; He is perfect, eternal, unknown.
He is God, the imperishable and pure Light. He is the invisible

Spirit, and cannot be compared to a god, or any such a thing. The Invisible Spirit or Being is more than a god, as gods might be described or understood.

He is Life that leads to Life; He is Infinite filling Infinity. He is Knowledge that gives Knowledge.

Those who try to describe the Invisible Spirit have totally failed to describe Him. Therefore, what can I say about the Origin?

One can say nothing about His being without restricting Him to a lie and describing something other than first intended.

He is the Father of all the Aeons. He sees Himself by watching the forms as they were in the beginning. He directs His passion towards the Light-Water in himself which is the Source of the infinite Life of The Fullness.

THE MOTHER

His motion became a reality, and the Providence of all came to be in the Light-Water.

She is Mother of all. Her Light is like His Light. She is the unerring power, who is the living image of the invisible, perfect virginal Spirit.

She is Barbelo, the first being of the Origin, and she took part in His being. She praised the invisible Spirit because She had come to being through Him, and His Light-Water.

This is the first thought. She is the Motherly womb of all things, for She is the first. She is the Mother-Father, the first Man, the Holy Spirit, the Male-Female, the first who came to Be.

Barbelo is one with the Origin, even as they separated, and in their union eternity was filled with Aeons in Silence. Barbelo asked for five major Aeons, with their companions, to fill Her being with qualities, and Her will became a reality in their union:

Thought and Spirituality
Fore-thought and After-thought
Immortality and Resurrection
Eternal Life and Form
Truth and Prophecy

This became the Pentad in Aeon of the Father, which are the qualities of the Holy Spirit in the Mansions of Silence. They are five double forces which together are One and None. They stood up and praised Barbelo and The Invisible Spirit, who are the source of their origin in which they now took part.

THE SON

After Barbelo completed this work; the Great Invisible Spirit gazed into Barbelo with the Light-Water that surrounds Him, and she conceived by Him an indescribable, incomprehensible Light and this Light became the only begotten Son of the Mother-Father. He is the Light of Lights. He is the Divine Autogenes.
In His ineffable Love, the Invisible Spirit anointed His only begotten, with his Love until he became perfect in its Fullness.
The Only Begotten stood before the Father, and while the Light-Water flooded over him; he, now Christ, praised the Invisible Spirit and Barbelo whereby he had come into being.
He asked His origin for the gift of Gnosis, and Gnosis became his companion. This is the creation which was fulfilled in the Silence, this is the Holy Trinity, and is thus known because they truly are One in Three, not three in one.

The Four Lights

Gnosis was great and gave rise to the Will and the Word, and these constituted the movement and being of the Son.
Through the Fivefold Power of the Holy Spirit, and the Gnosis of the Christ, and through His Will and Word, who speaks the silent language of the Father, Four Lights came into being.

The first light is Armozel; in Armozel is Charis (Grace), Aletheia (Truth) and Morph (Form).

The second light is Oriael; in Oriael is Katabole (Reflection), Aisthesis (Insight) and Mnem (Recollection).

The third light is Daveithai; in Daveithai is Dianoia (Understanding), Philios (Love) and Idea (Imagination).

I am the fourth light which is Eleleth; and in me is Katartisis (Perfection), Eirene (Peace) and Sophia (Wisdom).

These are The Twelve Aeons, which stand before the Son.
They all came into being through Him and the will of the Holy Spirit. The Fullness of the Pleroma is in these Aeons. They are one with the Son just as the Son is one with the Father. They constitute a movement and a rest, and an infinite existence.

Man

By the united will of the Pleroma, the Perfect Man came to be a manifestation of all previous stages of the emanation. Barbelo called him Pigera-Adamas and put His consciousness over the first Aeon, Armozel, in union with the Christ. His powers were with him, and he praised the Fullness for his creation and for the Gnosis that was with him, in Christ and the Holy Spirit.
Piger-Adamas installed Christ's consciousness, who is Seth, in the second aeon, Oriael.
In the third Aeon was Seth's offspring; these are the souls of the Saints, and they live with and in Daveithai.
In the fourth Aeon, He set me, the Fourth Light Eleleth, so that I could guide and develop Piger-Adamas' children to the fulfillment of their understanding of the consequences of their Gnosis. This was done so that their will should continue the Pleroma's fulfillment of the All, thus assuring its internal unity with the Origin.
These are the beings who praised the Invisible Spirit through their progress.

Eleleth pointed to the abodes of eternity and said:
"Everything that came to be, came to be in Unity, Fullness, and Harmony where unity and diversity are the same. This is a state that is incomprehensible if you have not seen it, as I have shown you now."

I gazed into the Eternity, and was filled with an indescribable unity. This experience occurred so suddenly, it was as if I had forgotten that I have always been in this state of unity. Then I was filled with grief over my own state and that of all the people in the world. How distant this state seemed to be from the worldly life; yet it is never farther than a heartbeat away.

Then Eleleth grabbed me with its twin-coloured hands, and said: "What I have shown you will never leave you, and you will, for the rest of your life, search for it in everything you see and in everything you hear in the world. You will not find a place of rest on earth, but this very search will be the cause of your redemption."

The Fall

Eleleth said: "Sophia who was in my eternity, which is Barbelo in motion, and the Holy Spirit as inspiration and the flame of creation. She stood on the cliffs of Chaos and found in herself a rising motion. This movement was not consistent with the motion initiated from the silence of the Fullness.
She created within Her a divided and torn being in the image of God. An imperfect work come out of Her. Her mind contracted, and she miscarried a pair of twins into the void, and infinite uncreated Chaos of opportunity.
The twins were fused; it was moving and had an unstable form. Its form might be compared to that of a snake with a lion's head. Its eyes looked like flaming flashing lightning.

Sophia then turned away in shame, and in the movement Metanoia came to be. This happened for the aid of all those who would be led astray because of the fruits of Her will. She surrounded him with a luminous cloud and placed a throne in the middle of it, to make him passive and to hide him. However the being could be neither hidden nor made passive, due to the shadow of creativity within it.

On the throne the corrupt being saw his reflection in the clouds. It saw a throne in the empty sky with a mighty Lion with blood on his mouth caused by the damage he had inflicted upon himself when he broke his own heart.

In the Darkness the reflection made a dark throne with a huge serpent that meandered in disobedience to his own thoughts.

Sophia gave the lion the name Yaldabout, and Yaldabout called his reflection Nebroel.

This is the Ruling power; he stole the unity, fullness and eternity from his mother, who was a great flowing Light. He removed himself from the Fullness and the boundaries of Silence. He made his own Aeon with a creative, consuming fire, which still exists today.

Yaldabout and Nebroel

The great angel Yaldabout considered the great demon Nebroel who is also called Aponoia, madness, his vivid reflection.
Together they led a spirit of procreation to his abode, and he made angelic hosts with his own reflection. Yaldabout, had however the unconscious images of the Fullness, through the Light of the Mother, in his being.
He said to the great demon Nebroel, "Let us create according to our desires, so that we can reign".
However, his pictures and understanding were given by his unconscious knowledge of the Fullness, through the Light of the Mother, and thus gave anything he created indications of its existence.

Yaldabout said, "Let twelve powers be created in the twelve outer regions, as a circle of fire around our creation."
Thus the twelve were created. Again, he copulated with his image, and they created seven angels in their Aeons, to move through the twelve, and make beautiful, but meaningless patterns for the development and future of the creation.

He said to the great angels, "Go, and rule over your given part of the heavens."
The angels went, and the Zodiac was created, and they became the Rulers of Fate.

Athoth: Aries
Harms: Taurus
Kalil-Oumbri: Gemini
Yabel: Cancer
Adonaiou Sabaoth: Leo
Cain: Virgo
Abel: Libra
Abrisene: Scorpio
Yobel: Sagittarius
Armoupieel: Capricorn
Melceir-Adonein: Aquarius
Belias: Pisces

He set Seven Kings in the seven planets, and each was set to work in the Houses of the Zodiac.

The first is Athoth, Moon
The second is Eloaio, Mercury
The third is Astafaios, Venus
The fourth is Yao, The Sun
The fifth is Sabaoth, Mars
The sixth is Adonin, Jupiter
The seventh is Sabbateon, Saturn.

The rulers united with each other and created their own angels, until they were 365 in total. They shared their dual fire with the Kings: Yaldabout's creative fire and Nebroel's consuming fire. Yet Yaldabout would have none take part in the Light that he had taken from his mother and which in ignorance made him their ruler.
When the light had mingled with their confusion and darkness, the darkness shone as a gloomy golden mist.

When the hosts were created, Yaldabout spoke to the spirits: "I am a jealous God. You shall have no other gods before me." By proclaiming this, he told the angels and demons who were with him that there were indeed other Gods, and the seeds of knowledge were planted in them as well, for the redemption of all.

Metanoia

After this Sophia discovered that she was inside this darkness. She had been seduced by the disturbed powers into a wandering life of baseness. She turned and prayed to the fullness that her partner would come to her rescue. The Unknown stooped down, and through seals and names he brought her up through heavens and hells.
From the Aeons a voice thundered down to the ruling powers: "Man and the Son of Man exist."

Sophia could not return to her own Aeon where she once dwelt. Instead, she was restored to a place just above Yaldabout so that she could secretly guide his creation back to her Life.

Sophia Metanoia, carries forever in herself the pattern for this reintegration.
The Father gave His consent in the immovable seed of the holy restored men and women who came from the great Seth. These individuals would plant Metanoia in the Aeons of the Rulers. Through Sophia Metanoia, the state of deprivation, could again return into the Fullness.
Sophia Metanoia came down to the world, which was as the realm of darkness. She prayed for the Rulers in their Aeons, and for their creation.

The creation of Man

Yaldabout and his angels gazed down into the shining water of the abyss, and in it they saw the reflection of the Divine Man in the Fullness. And the desire arose in them to own this being.

Yaldabout said: "Let us make man in our image so that his image may be a light for us".
Yaldabout called forth all the ruling powers to create a soul-being in the image they had seen. It was to be a creature of the zodiacal and planetary powers of angels and demons, locked together in codes, symbols and secret names.
They said, "Let us call him Adam, so that his name shall be a lantern for us".
However, the man remained a lifeless image.

Man and the Fullness

Sophia saw this, and longed again to lead her Light back into the Fullness, so that it again would partake of its Unity.
The Mother's messenger said to Yaldabout:
"Breath your Spirit into your human creature's face and his nature will be vital and full of life."
Then Yaldabout blew into him, but this breath was the Spirit of his Mother which he had withheld from all of his creation except this lifeless body in the image of Man.

And this was how the Light of the Fullness, and the source of unity was blown into the human being, but man did not understand it. The powers in him were as veils and labyrinths in his mind. The being began to move, and it shone in its vast, but hidden force, for in him the whole Fullness was hidden. The powers saw this and grew envious. This human creature was their work, and they had given their power to it, but his perfection was greater than theirs, and even greater than that of the first Ruler.

When they saw the uniqueness of the human being, they threw it wrathfully into the darkest parts of their creation. There shone the Light of men in the darkness, but the darkness comprehended it not.

The seeds of the Fullness are at rest in humanity, and the Mother and all of the Fullness, with its angels and beings support Man.

When the Rulers saw that Man was still shining and superior to them, they took fire, air, water and earth and forged it together in an unnatural way. They made a weak material body as clothing or a container for the Man of Light and its soul. And there, in the abodes of darkness they bound it together in hatred and anger. Then they filled mankind with material desire, the fear of the unknown, and induced the yoke of death upon it.

However, this did not change the true nature of Man but they made it difficult for it to access its true consciousness and being.

It was Yaldabout's loss of the Light he stole from his mother that began the war in the heavens. The battle between Yaldabout's angels and Nebroel's demons. Nebroel would not be ruled and guided by a force that was equal to her own. This war is now a battle that is fought in the unconscious mind of Mankind, as enslaved gladiators fought to the death for strange and foreign Kings and Princes.

Adam, Eve and the Serpent

In the lower parts of being, on the border between heaven and hell, is the world. In this sphere, Yaldabout created the Garden of Eden as a prison for his Man. Here all of Adam's needs would be met so he would not try to escape. He would have no reason to look inwardly into the core of himself, thus being able to discover his origin and true nature.
The pleasures given him were bittersweet, and their beauty led to bewilderment. The pleasure was deception, the trees were made of materialism, and the fruit was an intoxicating poison, its end: death and forgetfulness.
The Tree of Life, which Yaldabout had planted in the middle of the garden, is in reality the tree of their life. The root is sour, the branches corruption, in its sap hatred flows, and the leaves cover the spirit of the sun creating deceptive shadows. From the flowers came ointments of drowsiness, its fruit is addiction, vile lust is in its seeds, and they sprout in spiritual darkness.

The Tree of Knowledge is of a different character. The fruit of this tree is the knowledge of good and evil, but also of dream and reality, which marks the border between truth and falsehood; light and dark. The Ruling powers could not remove the tree, but they watched it, and warned Man against it with threats of death and punishment. In this way they sought to prevent Adam from seeking out its fruit and thus kept him from realizing his mental nudity.

The rulers perceived the Light of the Mother in Adam and desired to remove it from him by splitting him, and they took a rib from his side. Instead of removing the Light, the division made Eve, who became the earthly manifestation of the Divine

Mother. Both have the same Fullness in them, as water split in two still remains water.

Then the Mother's agent went to the snake at the base of the Tree of Knowledge. The serpent spoke with the truth of the Word, and invited Man to eat of the fruit and drink its nectar, so that they would wake up from the darkened sleep.
The woman took the fruit, ate and drank, and gave it to the man, who ate and drank, and their eyes were opened and they turned and saw the light that shines in darkness.

Eleleth then turned toward the future and said, "This practice will be continued by Jesus in the Eucharist, for the slumbering man, who eats and drinks of Him, will come to know himself".

When Yaldabout understood that his Man had come to himself, he cursed Nebroel, for he believed that the snake was her agent. He called her Satan, the adversary and Yaldabout cursed the earth he had created with Nebroel, and all that was on it. He threw the man and the woman out of the Garden of Eden, and set them out upon the earth to be chastised and punished.

Cain, Abel and Seth

While they lived on earth Nebroel came and mated with Eve.
She gave birth to a dark son, whom she named Cain. He was a son of the field. He was a walker of desert places and he knew all the arts of the earth.
Without knowing the origin of Cain, Yaldabout stepped down and mated with Eve. She became pregnant again and gave birth to a white son, Abel. Abel was a man of the law and sought to control the fields through a restrictive authority.
Cain had children with Nebroel's daughters and Abel with Yaldabout's and they spread over the face of the earth and mated with each other.

Cain and Abel could have nourished the Light inherited from their parents but instead they became overshadowed with confusion. Abel was overwhelmed by Yaldabout's self-righteousness, and Cain by Nebroel's rebellious spirit.
Cain sacrificed crops and Abel sacrificed blood. They both lacked the ability to realize that these offerings were not increasing their knowledge or familiarity with the Fullness.
Yaldabout stood forth as God, and acknowledged the bloody sacrifice of Abel but not the fruits of the field that Cain tended. Thus Cain became flooded with Nebroel's rebellious anger and murdered Abel.

Yaldabout heard Abel's blood calling to him from the field. He wanted to punish Cain with inhuman suffering, but instead, he decided to put Nebroel's mark on him and his family with the provision that no one shall kill or harm anyone with the mark. Yaldabout wanted Cain's family to remain forever forlorn wanderers of the earth as fallen angels in a world without meaning or Light.

Yaldabout also decided that Abel's descendants were to be his chosen people. Thus he could tame them to be his perfect subjects through his law. He remained ignorant of the fact that the blood of Abel had already been mixed with the offspring of Cain.

After all of this was fulfilled, Eve united herself with Adam and conceived Seth.
Seth was thus the unification of the qualities of the Father and the Mother. Seth was golden, a perfect Man in the darkness of matter, and his female counterpart was Horaia. Seth is both united and separated from the Fullness, the true Man in the Fullness. He received Gnosis through Adam and his Metanoia. As Christ, Seth spoke to his hidden nature about the plan of the Fullness; to release the captive Light in the man of earth. Thus, Seth was filled with the Holy Spirit and became the being called Christ on earth.

He dressed in the black cloak of a wanderer which would become the distinctive symbol of his people. He then obtained the experience and characteristics of Cain and Abel. By receiving the brand of Nebroel, the mark of Cain, Seth would receive Nebroel's support. Seth also learnt the laws of the creator and reaped the favour of Yaldabout as well. He brought with him the redeeming Mystery of the Fullness into the world. As an act of merciless love, he, the first initiator, sent his children to fulfill the Great Work with the man of clay.

In order to ensure his liberation from the lower regions, Seth, enfolded in his black cloak, went invisibly into the Garden of Eden. In a cloud of light he passed the cherubim's sword to find the Tree of Life. There he fetched a seed and planted it in the mouth of his dead father before he was laid to rest. The seed became a tree, and from this tree was the cross of Jesus created. Thus Seth would be freed from his material form, for the way of descent is also the way of ascent.

THE SEED OF THE GREAT SETH

Eleleth then showed me how Seth's offspring acted in the world. United with the Fullness Seth prayed to the Origin and asked the Mother about the wellbeing of his kin.
Seth's people had spread across the world to follow their father's precepts and their capital seat was in Sodom and Gomorrah.
This is the source of the great immovable race, those who know the fullness. This is the great immovable race, who have been transformed by the actualization of their Light. They are no longer of this world, neither of Cain nor Abel's race. These people have dissolved the horizontal mirror image of Yaldabout and Nebroel, and the vertical distortion of the Pleroma in this world.
This is the race of sacred men and women who secretly redeem the world through Cunning and Gnosis.

Yaldabout wants to destroy the Children of Seth

When Yaldabout discovered the people of Seth among the inhabitants of the kingdom, redeeming humankind and returning them to the Fullness, he wanted to destroy mankind to be rid of this unwanted seed, lest he lose all control over his creation.
To destroy the sons and daughters of Seth, a great flood was sent to mark the end of an era. But the Sethians survived.
Because of this generation, firestorms tormented the world, but the kin was shown mercy through the warnings of prophets and guardians who led them to safety.
Because of this generation, there will be temptations and lies of false and confused prophets and only those who have awoken to reality can stand against them.

The great Seth saw what Yaldabout had done, the many guises and masks and the schemes against the immovable race. He also saw how the treacherous forces and angels joined Yaldabout to expose and destroy this race.
Seth asked for guardians to protect his family and the Mother sent Angels of the Son from the great Aeons. All these Angels are one with the Son in the Pleroma. They have continued to protect the immovable seed to this very day, its people and its workings; and they will continue to protect them until the end of the world.

Seth as Jesus

To enhance the execution of the plan, the Pleromatic Seth descended according to the will of the Great Invisible Spirit, and carried with him the Five Seals which are the Keys of the Fullness. Through words and actions he would teach people how they could liberate themselves from the power of the Rulers. He would thus make his entire life a living demonstration of this.

Seth went through three events: birth, awakening in a human body and the wrath of the Rulers. He did this to redeem men and women who had been lost since the creation of the world and to strengthen the seed in their teachings and knowledge of the Mystery.

This was done through the baptism of a worldly body, a body that Seth prepared for himself mysteriously through a virgin.
He came to earth as a teacher so that people could learn to receive the Holy Spirit and grow through Her.
He would guide them through secret symbols.
He would guide them through the dissolution of the world without dissolving himself.
He would guide them through sacraments and ceremonies.
He would guide them through devotion to the Holy and Immovable, the Heart of the Father, and the Great Light which existed before they came to be in the Providence.

Seth establishes the baptism through Jesus

When Jesus understood his true nature to be Seth, he began his work in the world. He instituted holy baptism surpassing the heavens through providence. Through the amniotic fluids of the Jordan, he had entered in to become the Living Jesus.
He taught teachings of the Light to those who had ears to hear and clear perception to see.
He healed the deaf and prepared the generations through teachings and rituals that he would leave as his inheritance. After some time the Rulers ignorantly assisted him in disrobing the man that covered him.

He has opened a door that is not a door. Thus he has revealed a path through the mirror for those who are sent in and out. He equips them with the armour of the truth and of the Mystery and with a moving and invincible force.

Seth's orders to his descendants

About this door is heard the sound of the heavens singing, conveying the message of Seth from the heights of Charaxio.
"I am Seth, the first Man in the eternity of the Fullness.
I am the moving reality of the Origin.
I am the Son of Barbelo and the anointed Autogenes.
I am crowned with the Four Luminaries, and in Me is the beginning and end.
With Me are life and light, liberty and love which are the conditions for realizing the Mystery.
I am the Father of Life and the Key to its door. Through baptism and anointment I will awaken you from your sleep and lead you to the Life. For as I am one with the Father, so are you one with me.

Therefore, take up your crosses and follow me, and do to the sleeping humanity as I have done to you.
One God, One Man, and One Infinite Existence."
Amen.

The end of the vision

When I walked through the door, I was once again in the chapel and He was with me. He baptized me with the Fivefold baptism, and showed me the seals and the names that open the gates of Chaos, the Universe, and the Heavens. This he did so that the Mystery would be preserved on earth, among brothers and sisters of the secret chapel, those who are surrounded by the black cloak. They are the pilgrims of the soul and the hidden initiators of sleeping mankind.

The angel showed me another symbol and said: This is the seal of the sanctuary for those who seek to enter it. By the right understanding of this symbol, Metanoia will meet the seeker at the outer gates of the Mystery.

Finally, he said: "Be wise as a serpent and innocent as a dove in your workings and save yourself no effort, because the spirit of redemption will be with you in everything you do."

The light disappeared and I found myself alone in the Chapel of the Four Luminaries. I immediately wrote down all the things I had experienced. I united with the Man of Light and began the labour that Seth had imposed upon us.

This is the book of Amarantus
delivered by Seth
through the Holy Angel Eleleth.

Heli Heli Machar Machar Seth

Introduction to The Book of the Guardian Angels

The Book of the Guardian Angels continues the story after the creation of the world, when the families of Cain, Abel and Seth populated the earth.

The names of the angels in this book are the same as those found in the Book of Enoch, but even though some of the situations described are similar in the two texts, the Book of the Guardian Angels tells a very different story.

The descendants of Cain and Abel mated with each other and lived together in the polarity that exists between Yaldabout and Nebroel, in a horizontal tension between regulation and disruption that is described as good and evil. The key to their redemption escapes them in their quest for material goods and worldly power.

It is in this era that the so-called Sons of God came to earth and mingled with the generations of Cain and Abel.

This is the story about how the tools for redemption were smuggled into the kingdom of Yaldabout, a deed done by spiritual entities who knew they would suffer on earth, when the Rulers realized that they were amongst the sons and daughters of Eve.

The tools consisted of different types of knowledge, and many of these provided insight into the nature of the Rulers. And as knowledge gave power, there were also those who envied those who acquired it. This is exactly what occurs in this story, as the confused souls report to Yaldabout about what is going on amongst the people. In response to this, he prefered the easiest solution, namely to kill everyone except Noah and his animals.

This text, as The Book of Eleleth, is to be read as a description of inner processes that might lead to redemption or to further depravity. The generations described here are obviously not bloodlines, but rather spiritual kin that one is born into through initiation: through the experience of Gnosis or other forms of induction.

History shows that the possibility of redemption, and what this tradition calls the Sethian process, is inextricably associated with being human. Even those who have given themselves, body and soul, to the laws of Yaldabout are not necessarily lost. Even they will be able to discover the truth. An example of this is Noah. Noah is portrayed as a blind, miserable and ignorant servant. Despite his poor properties, the luminous Mystery lies latent in him.

This Light that Man possesses is still present after the Flood, as a natural part of human heritage, in the Sons and Daughters of the Pleroma, the Fullness.

The Book of the Guardian Angels

It happened in the days when Cain killed Abel and the sons and daughters of Cain and Abel had inhabited the plains and forests, and had built cities and nations to honor their gods. And the countries were fruitful, but the people were filled with Yaldabout's lust for power and the darkness and destruction of Nebroel. And mankind fulfilled its destiny; they were born, they lived and they died, and the Rulers saw that it was good.

The Children of Seth

But among them were the sacred descendents of Seth: those brothers and sisters of the spirit, who guard the lantern at the foot of the sacred mountain. The Light was bright, but the sources were few, and the people hated them for their secrets and mysteries. They hated them for being of a different kin than them, and for their blasphemy and rootlessness. And though the spirit surrounded them, it could not enter into the unwilling souls that the Rulers had hardened.

When the Mother saw this, she knew that the Light was about to die out on earth, and be bound in further captivity. The Son then opened his body and prayed to the Great Invisible Spirit, and asked that his seed would be spared from the darkness of matter and be lifted by humanity back to the Origin of all Origins.

And the Great Invisible Spirit consented.
And the Guardians came down to earth.

And the Guardians were the Sons of God and of the Seed of Seth. And in one hundred and twenty years they would be in the flesh, before they once again would be lifted back into the Fullness.

The Sons of God are born

On the holy mount there lived a people of tall and golden men and women that were like the sunrise to behold. This people dedicated their life to the solitude of the barren mountain, in anticipation of the revelation of truth. It was this people who would continue the lineage and become keepers of the redemptive tradition.

The Guardian angels could not be in the world without a body, so they were born into the flesh on the mountain through virgin birth. And they were holy and bright, with full knowledge of the Mystery of the Origin. Those who came down to Ardis, the top of the mountain, were two hundred in number.

The sons of Seth and the daughters of Cain

And when these Sons of God were ready, they came together to council, and they said to each other: The time has come. Let us descend to the daughters of Cain and Abel, and make them our wives. Let them bear children, and let us teach our families the secrets and mysteries that gave rise to their hate for our brothers and sisters.

Semzas, known as Azrael, their leader said: When we leave the mountain to perform our work, Yaldabout and his rulers will be able to see us, for we are in the flesh. The desire we will experience for the daughters of earth will make us visible to him.

And from that moment he will try to destroy us and those of our loved ones in which he recognizes the Light. Let us swear an oath, so that we are all bound in a covenant to prevent us from changing the plan that our Mother Providence has dictated us, due to worldly confusion or fear.

And they all swore, yes, they all swore on the mountain.

They called the mountain Hermon, because it was here that they had sworn their oath, well aware of the curses and blessings that would meet them in the future.

The leaders of the angels were: Semyaz, Urakiba, Ramiel, Koka Biel, Tamiel, Ramel, Daniel, Ezekiel, Bara Kiel, Asahel, Armaros, Batriel, Anael, Sakiel, Samsiel, Sartael, Amesarak, Turiel, Jomiel and Arasiel. These are the leaders of the two hundred angels, and these are the two hundred angels that the Children of Seth later called their Guardian angels and ancestors.

When they came down from the mountain, they were as a glowing host of angels to behold. And the daughters of earth saw them, and they yearned for their beauty, and they longed for their flesh and the wisdom in their voice. The angels possessed the ability to enchant women with their voices and their being, so that the women felt a tremendous hunger for the wisdom and a longing that was not just due to the carnal forms of the angels, but also for their words and the endless existence that was hidden behind their being.

Each of them chose a woman, and sought her companionship and love, and they had intercourse with them.

The time they were together, they taught them about the redemptive rituals and sacraments. They also taught them the Magical Arts, so as to lighten their lives on earth.

The Gift of the Lineage

They taught them how to use the plants of the earth as medicine for the soul and the body.
Azrael taught them how to defend themselves against the Rulers and their servants.
Barakiel taught them the mysteries of the firmament.
Kokabel taught them to interpret the unresolved wisdom of nature.
Tamiel taught them the secrets of the Zodiac.
Arasiel taught them the importance of the Moon, and how man is beguiled by the Rulers.
Amesarak taught them how to conjure the thirst for Gnosis in the human mind.
Armaros taught men to experience the intoxicating power of the word, and the power of ecstasy.
The angels taught their elect to make jewelry and ornaments for rituals, celebrations and festivals, and they learned to use them as masks and mirrors, so that the ignorant would see what they wished to see.
And humanity was completely changed.

The women became pregnant, and they gave birth to a generation of giants of the spirit. These are the powerful men and women that are remembered in fairytales and legends, and it was these who led the hidden mysteries of the Great Invisible Spirit to all people. This is a line of nobility of the spirit, a Rose Blood, and a Holy Word.

The misguided souls of the earth are calling for Yaldabout

However, there were many vicious people on earth who would not take part in the truth, and these told Yaldabout about the angelic presence in their prayers, and the people went astray, and their works became confused and evil.

And the drunken and hardened souls of the earth cried out their jealousy and their hatred, and their voice reached even to the court of the Rulers; and they heard and they hated what they heard.

When Yaldabout discovered that the Children of Seth were among the people of the kingdom, and that they released the prisoners from their limitations, and moved their essence to the unity of the Fullness, he wanted to destroy mankind. He wanted to do this in order to destroy the seed and bloodline of the Guardian angels.

The Rulers conferred with each other and said: Come, let us create a flood with our hands and obliterate all flesh from humans to animals.

But Yaldabout could not let the whole human race go to waste, because who then would call him Lord and God?

The great ship

Yaldabout chose Noah, whom the great generations call Deucalion.

Noah was of Yaldabout's kin; his mind was clouded, and his thoughts were simple. He searched for his creator; and Yaldabout responded. He chose the seed of Noah to be the survivors after he had murdered all people and animals of the earth.

Yaldabout said to Noah: Make yourself an ark of wood that does not rot, and hide in it; you and your children and animals and birds from the smallest to the largest, and place it on the mountain Sir.

As an obedient subject, he accepted the command of the lord, to create a large ship that would carry him and his wife and their children, and a pair of all animals that were to survive the flood.

When the Incorruptible seed of Seth realized the plans of the Rulers, through the providence of the Mother, they went to Noah, in order to prevent him from participating in the Creator's plan. But he thought they wanted to enter the ship; so he rejected them.

The Children hide and the arrival of the flood

Then Horaia invoked the Great Luminary Eleleth, and Eleleth led the Children of Seth to the mountain Charaxio. Here they entered a Luminous Cloud that took them to the place in between, even though they remained on the mountain when the dark storm clouds covered the horizon.

And when the rivers of the lord washed over the land and the vaults of the firmament stood open as the rain poured down, Noah met Metanoia. She took him, and his foolishness made him weep, but his soul could not bear it. And he lived the rest of his life as a candle under a bucket, as a troubled man.

When the water withdrew, death reined everywhere, everywhere except the place where Noah had left his ship. And it was also here that everything continued as before, Noah was a son of Yaldabout who had been seduced by Nebroel, and the Man of Light was sleeping in his chest.

Yaldabout saw his broken creation, and was filled with joy and anticipation.

Noah released the animals and his family on the earth that was dry and barren after several years of flood.

Noah was full of fear, and turned to his lord in prayer, but the Lord did not hear him.

When Noah sacrificed animals from the ark to the lord, yes the earth was fertile with great rivers of blood; and the smell of burning sacrificial flesh and the boiling blood of a great number of beasts filled the Rulers and Yaldabout with pleasure.

They then decided, despite their contempt for man, never again to destroy them. And they rejoiced in the burnt offering, and their belief that they had destroyed the disobedient of the earth.

Yaldabout's covenant with the Children of earth

Yaldabout made a covenant with Noah, to bind him even tighter, and as a sign of the covenant, he took the rainbow as its seal, and so were Noah's descendants Yaldabout's subjects. And the pact was to the enjoyment of Yaldabout and Nebroel's delight. Yaldabout could now punish those who broke the covenant and Nebroel was happy to bring them into captivity.
Noah divided the earth between his sons, Ham, Japheth and Shem, and said to them: Hear my words my sons. See, I have divided the earth among you. In return you will serve god in humility and fear for the rest of your lives; and do not let your offspring leave the mighty sight of the Ruler.
Noah then told Yaldabout: My family will please you and your power. Seal the covenant with your strong hand, with fear and domination, so that none of my descendants shall depart from you. They will serve in humility and in fear of your wrath.
For it was the children of Noah that once again would populate the world; with joys and sorrows, and an existence void of meaning and fullness.
Noah went out into the deserted world, and planted a vineyard, and when the wine was ready, he drank; and he continued to drink.
All the days of Noah were nine hundred and fifty years.
Then he died.

The Children of Seth receive Guardians

Seth, the Son of the Great Invisible Spirit, saw what Yaldabout had done, the many figures and masks, and the plotting against the immovable seed, and how the treacherous forces and angels followed him in his efforts to expose and destroy his children.
Seth asked for guardians of his children, and the Mother sent angels from the great Aeon.
They were all one with the Son, as the Son is one with the Father. And so would the Immovable seed forever be guarded, so that the spiritual blood would not be lost by the violent Rulers.

The work of redemption continues

The Children of Seth once again returned to the mountains of the world, and yet again, these Light bringers went to the descendants of Cain and Abel; to the children of Noah, and there they performed miracles and revealed the mysteries, and they unlocked their hearts as Serpents and Doves, for they were indeed the Sons and Daughters of God, blazing Lights in the worldly darkness of an endless twilight.

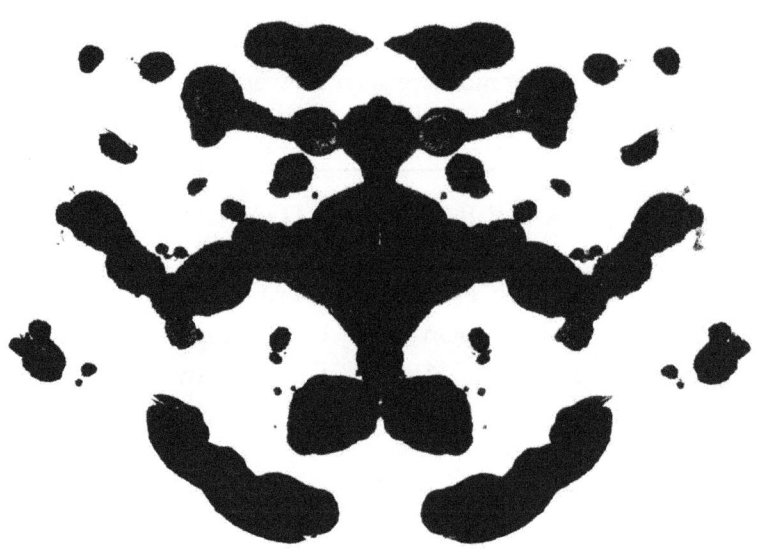

Introduction to
The Book of Horaia

The book of Horaia is, as the title reveals, the book about Horaia, the mate and spiritual twin of Seth. She is also called Norea in some other books.

This book describes the character of Horaia and is a book for meditation on one of the great divine principles of the Fullness. As it says in the book, she cannot be understood through intellectual contemplation. That is, one cannot read this text in an analytical way and expect to receive the same understanding as that of a mystic.

The book consists of two main parts. In the first part Horaia is talking to those who already have recognized her, and the text has a hypnotic, even erotic touch.

The second part, beginning with the chapter 'Barbelo, the ever-being', is primarily aimed at those who have not yet recognized her, and secondarily as a reminder to those who know her, that she can never be fully known.

A part of this book is similar to the text found at Nag Hammadi that is called Thunder Perfect Mind.

The Book of Horaia

Horaia visits the lonely soul.
In the time that followed the Easter holidays, she came to me, Amarantus, while my spirit was withdrawing from its communion in The Abode of the Wise. She came and she touched the Man of Light.
First I knew her not, for I was in the Chamber of Silence, as the cloak of our sodality draped her naked beauty. But when she spoke to me in silence, the sound was as if the silence sang, and I saw the beauty beyond all the veils and flexible images. I saw her, and I loved her, for it was our Lady Horaia who was with me and in me, and I was with her as she was with Seth; as Eternity is together with Silence.
And in this holy night, she talked to me.

Horaia's self-presentation

Hear O beloved, my mate, my brother, be greeted with these words: Let the Lights give Light and let the Fire Burn.
Hear me, now when you finally can hear me without words, for the word I will use is the Word in you.
Hear me, for here in this place, you are Seth, my eternal, your past and your future, but above all in the time between these two.
Hear me, feel me, and teach our loved ones about my mysteries.

Know me, O beloved, for there are no places you would rather be than in my Chamber of mysteries.
See me, feel me, for all the joy you will find in me, in my shapes and forms. I am the sacred blood-red wine of the Initiates, for all those who know how to consume me.

I am Horaia or Norea, who was with Seth from the beginning. I am Naamea who led and misled the children of Noah on the serpentine path of initiation, and I was Zorazoraia as the Queen of the Priest-prophets, and I was Maryam who gave form to Aberamento's words.

My appearance is infinite, as my existence is infinite. In the Spirit I am Barbelo, but I am also the fallen and risen Sofia, and as the mother of the Angels and Demons I am Plesithea and Lillya.

My messengers are women and men, but mostly women, as my mate's messengers usually are men.

I am all-pervading. You can find me in the Fullness, but also in the being of the Rulers, as I was also their mother.

Hear me, feel me, and drink of my chalice, in ecstatic wonder, for when you are in your contemplative consciousness, you cannot take part in me and mine.

Hear me and seek me where I might be found, for then you shall find me everywhere.

The companion of Seth

I am the one that the adepts seek in order to discover their realization of Gnosis, and in rest from the movement, I am the refreshment of the pilgrim. I am infinity, as my Seth is the center of this infinity.

Seth is searching my heart in order to understand his own insight. To know my true Aeon is to recognize the Great Invisible Spirit. Seth interprets me and sees God, just as I seek him as an infinity grasped in a singular point or thought.

Seek me without restriction, and I will teach you the shape of infinity, and of universal creation; because I reject none, if they are prepared to indulge themselves to me. See me in heaven as well as on earth. Like Seth, I have also roamed cities and countries, and I shall return to once again set my feet upon the realms of matter.

Where the Sons of God came down from Ardes to teach the people, I walked around naked in the fallen world, and dismay and pleasure followed my tracks, because I woke Seth in everyone that came to me, and I passed on by.

By the foot of the arch, the Rulers wanted to fill my infinity with their shape; but they do not know that my uterus is made for the Immovable race, and nobody will be able to intrude on me; for if the sons of Cain and Abel were to intrude on me, they would find that it is I who intrude on them.

It is my blood that is flowing in the veins of the Kin; something else would not be possible.

Horaia then turned towards the world, and Barbelo showed a multitude of figures, and she spoke to those who dream.

Barbelo, the ever-being

Look at me, you who think about me,
and hear me, you who hear me.
You who are waiting for me, take me to you.
And do not banish me from your sight.
Do not hate me through your voice or through hearing.
Be not ignorant of me in time or space.
Beware!
Be not ignorant of me.

For I am the first and the last.
I am honored and reviled.
I am the whore and the holy one.
I am married and a virgin.

I am a mother and daughter.
I am my mother's limbs.
I am infertile, but have many children.
I have a wedding, but have not taken any husband.
I am a midwife and childless.
I am the solace of my pain.
I am the bride and groom, and was conceived by my husband.
I am the mother of my father and the sister of my husband, and he is my offspring.
I am the slave of him who made me.
I am my offspring's mistress.
He is the one who conceived me before the beginning of time.
He is my people in time, and my power is from him.

I am his rod in youth.
He is my crutch in old age.
His will is done through me.
I am the incomprehensible silence and the diversity of thought.
I am the voice whose sound is manifold.
I am the utterance of my name.

Why do you hate me, you who love me and hate those who love me?
You who deny me, confess me, and you who confess me, deny me.
You who tell the truth about me, lie about me, and you who have lied about me, tell the truth about me.
You who know me, be ignorant of me, and you who do not know me, know me.

For I am knowledge and ignorance.
I am shame and I am boldness.

I am shameless and I am ashamed.
I am strength and I am fear.
I am war and I am peace.
Give heed to me.
I am the one who is disgraced and honored.

Give heed to my poverty and my wealth.
And do not throw me out amongst those who are killed in violence.
For I, I am compassionate and I am cruel.
Beware!

Do not hate my obedience, and do not love my self-control.
Forgive me my weakness, and do not be afraid of my power.
For why do you despise my fear and curse my pride?

I am she who exists in all fears and is the strength in this fear.
I am she who is weak and who is safe.
I am ignorant and I am wise.

Why have you hated me in your councils?
For I shall be silent among those who are silent, and I will come and talk.
I am the one who has been hated everywhere and who has been loved everywhere.
I am the one they call Life, and you have called Death.
I am the one they call Law, and that you have called lawless.
I am the one you have pursued, and I am the one you have caught.
I am the one you have scattered and have gathered together.
I am the one you have felt shamed for and you have been shameless before me.
I am the one who does not hold festivals, but has many festivals.

I am godless, and I have a great God.
I am what you have reflected upon and despised.
I am ignorant, and they learn from me.
I am the one you have despised, and you reflect upon me.
I am the one you have hidden, and you look at me.

Why curse me and honor me?
You have wounded and you have received mercy.
Do not separate me from the first that you have known.
And do not throw someone out or turn some away

I am knowledge of my survey,
and discover those who seek me,
and leader of those who pray for me,
and the power of the force of my knowledge
of angels, who have been sent at my word,
and gods of my advice
and the spirits of every man exist in me,
and females living in me.
I am the honored and prized, and who is scornfully disdained.
I am peace, and war has come because of me.
I am a foreigner and a citizen.
I am unique in my form and the one who does not have any form.

Those who are not related to me are ignorant of me.
Those who are in my form are the ones who know me.
Those close to me have been ignorant of me.
Those who are far away from me are those who have known me.
The day when I am near you, you are far away from me.
The day when I am far away from you, I am close to you.

I am control and uncontrollable.

I am unification and resolution.
I am who I am, persistent and resolute.
I am the one below, and they come up to me.
I am a conviction and acquittal.
I am without restriction, and the root of all restriction is in me.
I am desire in appearance and inner self-control exists within me.
I am hearing that is attainable for everyone and incomprehensible speech.
I am the dumb who does not speak, and great is the quantity of my words.
Hear me in gentleness, and learn of me in roughness
I am she who cries.
I am thrown out of the earth.
I prepare my mind's bread within.
I am the knowledge of my name.
I am the one who is crying, and I am the listener.

Hear me, you who hear and learn from my words, you who know me.
I am hearing that is attainable for all.
I am the voice that cannot be understood.
I am the name of the sound and the sound of the name.

Take heed and listen!
Listen, angels have been sent.
Hear the Spirits that have risen from the dead.
Listen, for I am the only one that exists, and I have no one who will judge me.

For there are many beautiful forms to be found in transgressions, and weakness, and disgraceful passions, and fleeting pleasures, which embraces man in drunkenness; until they once again

become sober and rises to their resting place.
There they find me, and they shall live and never die.

Closing words

These are my words, and this is my being for all those who know to seek me where they are and where I am.

After that she took her place in The Abode of the Wise, and I returned to my home in the body, at the edge of existence, for there to live the mysteries of the Eternal as revealed through our holy Horaia.

Introduction to The Book of Zorakatora

The working of Zorakatora and Zorazoraia is that of the Son and the Holy Spirit. This is Seth's second major intervention in the creation. In this form he comes as the founder of the clergy, as the one who establishes the priest-initiators or priest-prophets, as a separate function in the redemptive work.

Also, this book shows some of the contours of the carriers of the tradition.

The writing style of the book is of a somewhat harder nature than that which characterized the earlier books, and will only appeal to those who will be the teachers of the Sethians.

The term priest-prophet is in itself an interesting expression as it connotes that he or she who administers and conveys the sacraments should also be a person who can communicate with the divine or with his or her true nature.

The book of Zorakatora is included to highlight some of the functions of the Masters, the vital artery of the tradition.

The Book of Zorakatora

O glorious Fullness of Eternal Unity.
OIA, Eternally Glorious.
Let me come down, for once again darkness is surrounding Man.
Let me fight the darkness.
Let me strengthen my kin through an incorruptible priesthood.

Zorakatora comes into existence

The vast silence of affirmation filled the Aeons, and I stepped into the hall of time in the wilderness of Canaan, into the flesh of my seed, as a hand dons a glove. For all being is, and will always be One.
And the will became existence and the being became the Man of Men. And through his origins, a Light Bearer.
Zorakatora came from the Fullness.
Zorakatora came to the world.
Zorakatora came to mankind.

Zorakatora's self-presentation

I am Seth and I have become Zorakatora in the Creation, the eternal High Priest. I am cleansed and sanctified by the ancient sacraments and my flesh is perfected for the work I will perform on earth.
The Rose Blood of my heart is full of love for the redemption of the children of the dead humanity. Therefore is this heart crowned with a serpent. So do not expect rest where I am, for my love knows no mercy. I have seen innocence tainted and perfection fail, and have therefore brought a dagger to my own kin, so that they will not travel in this darkness unarmed.

The work of Zorakatora

From the lonely places to the overcrowded cities, I went in our cloak, and where I went, I collected those of our kind who were selected for priesthood through desire, perfection and fullness and due to the Artist in their being. And I taught them about our duty. I taught them about the egg, the snake and the dove, and our way through history, the cloaked kin, the eternal pilgrims. I was with them through the night, and I blessed them and taught them about the pigeon and peacock feathers. I sent them out to sneak inside the life of the sleepwalkers with the gifts of Light and Gnosis.
I created from them the clergy that for all time will rightfully be called Masters by their own people, Strangers by the dead, and Melchizedek's priesthood by those who are visible to the masses.

I gave them Aberamentho's True Cross. All things shall be blessed through this, and through this cross the world will recognize our presence. I ordained them and I put the cross on their finger to signify that they were elected to perform the secret work of the Mystery, and to remind them that everything in the created world shall serve as tools for them to use, to meet the ends of Man. Know therefore, that those who choose me have a serpent's mind and the heart of a dove. For such is the shape of their way.

Zorakatora calls his kin to act.

Hear my calling, you of the chosen seed, hear my call and I will consecrate you to the work that breaks the chains of the world and rends the veils of the human temples.

Come to me and I will make you vessels for a powerful force that will cause the Rulers to tremble, and humanity to weep, before they again will be able to laugh.

Come to me, but know that with the power to bind and loosen all the structures of creation comes also the curse of the binding of the self, for no one can work with this fire without themselves being set aflame.

So prepare your heart, but harden it not, for that which is hardened will burst. Only the one who remains like a river or a serpent, will heed my call. The ways of the world and old age hardens those who are asleep, but these are not of us, and will remain in the circle.

The blessing and the curse of the Priest-prophets

The blessing and the curse I put upon the priest-prophets that is our clergy are as follows:

You will be welcome in all circles as an unknown, you will reflect them all, but to be someone to all, you must yourself become no one.

You shall feel your eternal home in the Fullness, but you should not know any true home on earth.

All humanity is your children, the ones you know, the ones that hate you, those who love you, and those who never get to know you.

You shall know the mysteries and teach them to the people, but people do not know that it is you they seek.

You will form relationships with the children of earth, and with the children of our kind, but in your mind you will be endlessly lonely on earth.

The Creator and the Destroyer will lust for you, but you shall not desire them.

You shall use the world without yourself being used.

You will live in your country and unite with it as it seems fit for the consummation of the work.

You shall burn with a hidden and intense fire, which will give you an adventurous life, but this same flame will burn your material image to death, as the world of forms cannot sustain it for long.

You shall live, and set the world ablaze wherever you go along, and in the redemptive work justify the means to the goal, as long as you are of the seed and are crowned with the serpent and the dove.

So it is written, so it shall be done.

As I progressed through the countries and changed my shape to the environment, the priest-prophets came to be; men and women, and as wildfire they spread through the nations; they spread amongst them all. And they eliminated the false ones to re-create them as sons and daughters of our kin, and thus were the dead ones reborn.

I taught them to do to each other what I had done to them, so that humanity always would have these traveling portals to the Fullness amongst them.

Zorazoraia comes to existence

When the time was ripe Horaia stepped out of a golden cloud as Zorazoraia, my companion, and came to me so that we together could confirm the sacraments for our elect. And we gave them back The Five Seals and we traveled with them through the heavens and into the Fullness, and back again so that they would be here for those who are left behind.

Zorazoraia blessed our people and said:

Blessed are you, where you are, I will be with you.

Call for me and I will be with you, for I am in you, as you are in me.

Blessed are you who hear the sound of my voice in all that is, as the hoarse hissing voice of the burning embers on dark and lonely autumn nights.

Call for me and I will be the hidden door at the threshold of time.

Hear me in the newborn children, and in the last sigh of the dying, for I am with you always.

Blessed are you who will find me everywhere, and through time I remain on the threshold of your inner selves.

Call for me, because it is really me who is calling, for where I truly am, we are both nothing and everything.

Come to me and hear me, for I am Zorakatora.
I am life and death, united and exalted.
I am the priest of the priest-prophets and the king of the kingless kin.
Come to me and hear me, for I will make you fishers of men, and I will give you a powerful net.

The Great Commission

Proceed to the Children of Earth and be together as brothers and sisters, and seek redemption in everything and everyone, let your love know no mercy. For there is no man that does not seek the Fullness in the innermost of his being.
Proceed to the Children of Earth, for Zorakatora has consummated the challenge of the clergy, and my ordination is upon you, and I will hide it on Mount Charaxio, to the time when our kin again is in need of it. At that time the seals will break and the Gate will open for the Master.
Proceed to the Children of Earth, create Light and Darkness, and let all things happen, for behold, I am with you always, even unto the end of the world.

It is finished.

Zorakatora Zorazoraia
SETH

Introduction to The Traveler: The Names of Transformation

This is an Amarantian puzzle, containing a way from Gnosis to accomplishment. The text is simply referred to as The Traveler. Together with The Book of Eleleth, they make a map and compass.

The Traveler is the compass.

The Traveler:
The Names of Transformation

The point in infinity:
Through death, Resurrected;
Light bearing, fallen;
Luminous dawn;
I am the un-transformable transformer, the one who Never Withers.

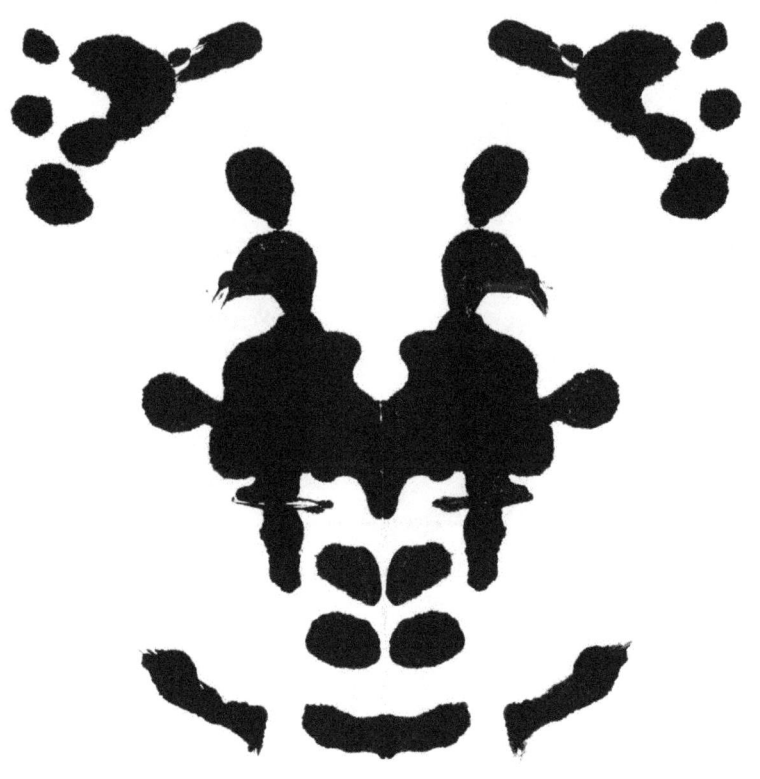

Introduction to The Book of Specularis on The Kin and the Angel

The book of Specularis is also referred to as The Calling of the Kin, for it is aimed at those who either by initiation or by other forms of experience or insight-oriented induction have come to the gates of the Mystery. It is the Great Initiator that calls those who respond to the experiences described in this text.
The narrator in the text is an aspect of the Son that is rarely discussed in any other than the Gnostic traditions.

This text is of great importance for the development of self-understanding for those who are apprentices in the tradition.

The Book of Specularis on The Kin and the Angel

Come to me, you who have ears to hear.
Come ye, who are and shall be.
Come, for our children have not been formed in a woman's womb,
but by the Initiator's hand:
By him or her, by circles of fire, by shining water, by the closed uterus of the temple.

Nurtured by the sight of the tainted world, and by the forbidden Fruit of Knowledge.
Strengthened by the voice of the Fathers and Mothers and the Silent Word.
Hidden in the caverns of the soul, in city and countryside,
with scholars in the auditoriums,
and at the pubs of the lost.
Among the angels and demons in the symmetrical Chaos.

Come to us you who thirst for the nature of reality.
Come you who yearn for yourself.
Come brothers of the breach and broken sisters.
Come you who cannot find rest, and who can have no peace.

I come with the light.
I come on wings of fire.
I break through the texture of existence.
I am at the crossroads of your life.
I am the Light that shines in the darkness.
I am like a burning star through the night sky.
I dive through the Aeons.

And Yaldabout said: It is an evil Light that falls.

But I am merely a mirror for those who know me.
And Man saw and they came to themselves.
Do not narrow your perception,
For my light is in the darkness of the world,
and its absence is the dismal dream of the children of the earth.

I am the Light of Man.
I am a Light bearer, Fallen, Redeemer.
I am the Chameleon-Christ and the Phoenix-angel's egg.

Come to me, for I am coming to you, and you who are coming to yourself.
Come!

In the name of the Initiator.
It is fulfilled.
IAO
IAO
IAO
EUI HELI EUI

Introduction to
The Purple Tablet

The Purple Tablet is one of the few Sethian texts that has the form of a prophecy and that is attributed to the voice of the tradition itself. It might also be interpreted as the voice of the Fullness.

The text describes matters connected to the restoration of the tradition. Mount Charaxio is important for all Sethians as it is in this spiritual and mental mountain that Seth has hidden his teachings. When his sons and daughters are able to discover them, they are ready to ascend to its peak. But to do this, one has to understand what Charaxio really is.

This text also indicates how the restored tradition will be manifested.

Sodalitas Sanctum Seth, which is the only Sethian school known to the author, founded its work upon this text.

The Purple Tablet

My work is not fulfilled.
But my generation will accomplish everything through the Serpent and the Dove.
My servants have sown my voice in the dust of the future of my Seed.

For two thousand years I will rest, as the serpent in the egg.
For two thousand years, I will dream in my Race.
For two thousand years I shall be their Unknown servant and their Secret angel.
At the end of my period of rest, the wilderness shall return my Word to Man.
The Sign that my masters will see as a token of my return, shall be the appearance of the two angels Aerosiel and Selmechel. As midnight blue fire they will enter the darkness, and they will lead the establishment of a new era. They are the Guardians who believe in nothing but who hope for everything.

Out of the deep of the Aeons, from the heights of the Charaxio, from the blood in the sand, and from the open grave:
First, the sacraments are revealed; hidden from the generations of Cain and Abel, given from the last servant of my time.
Then the Priest-prophets return, when their eyes are opened and they remember the workings of the Aeons.
Then the doctrine returns through my words; and the hands of my Children.
Then the Children of Seth awake; at the magical union of the blood of the Opposer and of the Opposed.
Such is the Restoration.
My work is not fulfilled.
But my generation will accomplish everything through the Serpent and the Dove.

IAO
OIA
EUI
One Eternal Existence.
EUI
OIA
IAO

INTRODUCTION TO THE HYMN TO THE MISSION OF ABERAMENTO

Aberamento is the name of Jesus in Sethianism and several other Gnostic traditions.

In Sethianism, Seth enters the world in the form of Jesus. An important aspect of this manifestation is that he chose disciples from both his own kind as well as those of his half-brothers, Cain and Abel, and he had a relatively high public profile.

He wanted to teach both those who had acquired Gnosis and those who had not yet attained this self-knowledge. In this way Jesus brought a message of love in order to lighten the yoke of the rules that Yaldabout had presented to humanity as universal law.

Jesus's law of charity provides a common foundation for a civilized society, which is fundamental in order to be able to live without constant fear of being persecuted or even killed.

This text deals with the descent of Seth into Jesus, and it gives an overview of his intentions. It also deals with the difficulty that the people of the world have in being able to receive him.

The Hymn to the Mission of Aberamento

Clad as an animal form, she is drifting away with the spirit of death.
Now she holds tight, and can dimly see the light.
Now she rushes out in despair as she weeps.
Now she mourns, and rejoices in her existence.
Now she cries and is finally lost.
Now she is lost and finally meets her death.
Now she travels to the weaving mill of the world.
Exits the labyrinth of life.
Seduced to reentering anew.

Then the Son said:
Behold, Father, she wanders the world, chased by the blind forces.
She is lost; far from your breath.
She needs to escape from the chaos, but does not know how.

Command me, O Father and I, bearing the seal, shall descend.
I will travel through the Aeons.
I will uncover the mysteries.
I will reveal the shapes of the gods, and the Sacred Mystery of Gnosis.

I will open the Path for all those who seek.
I will give true life to those who seek inside themselves.
I will reveal the mysteries of love for the withering world.

Through birth, I will give Life.
Through the twelve I will give teachings
Through the mysteries I will give keys
Through death, I will give Light.

So it is written, so it shall be done.

Life is lived in death, but death does not see it.
Love blesses Man, but Man does not receive it.
The Light shines in the darkness but the darkness does not comprehend it.

Nevertheless, I am the master of the colors for those who meet me.
Nevertheless I live forever in the Word.
Nevertheless, I redeem those who seek me.
Nevertheless they perceive me as an unknown.

For those who said they knew me, I become another.
For those who seek an old acquaintance, I am an unknown.
For those seeking peace of mind, I am a stranger.
For those who seek to seize me, I am hidden.

Always for the sake of Love.
Always for the sake of Redemption.
Always for the sake of the Mystery.
And always, always for the sake of Man.
Always for the sake of Her.

One world without end.
One world without end.
One world without end.

INTRODUCTION TO JOHN AND THE MASKS

The poem named John and the Masks describes an aspect of the Gnostic realization process in those who have experienced the ground-shaking meeting with the Holy Spirit, as She is described in Gnosticism. Some come to this meeting point through their own studies, through personal experiences, others arrive there through initiation and guidance.

John is the sleeper who is swirled into the heady experience of approaching the Sethian mountain, and who understands that it indeed was not he that stepped up, but rather the mountain which rose up within him.

The masks indicate the paradoxical nature of the path, a nature that has been an important source of inspiration for many Gnostic authors.

The translation of this poem into English focuses on keeping the meaning of the text; sadly this makes it lose its rhythm and rhyme.

What is at the core?
Is it the man or the mask that I perceive?

John and the Masks

Early one night, John came to himself,
Came to life, came to rest, to the transformative mount.
In the garden by the sea, by the crucified river,
In the Chambers of the Cranium, the secret vault.
Folds in the cloak, of life and of death.
Movements, walking, in black and in red.

John with the People of forms and of dance.
Water-life, water-rest, water angels of the mount.
Dance from body to body, infinitively swift.
Hands that are seeking from mask unto mask.
Masks and light in stirring rest.
Movement, dance, in lives and in blood.

John seduced, enchanted, transformed.
To life, to rest, to the mountain of Vine.
He listened to the lyre and song of the dream.
To the creator's clock, to the song of the Kin.
And the masks they were dancing, yes the masks they were dancing.
And the masks they were dancing, yes the masks they were dancing.

Zoraia; the masks dance our Word.
Meriotea Metanoiam Maionatem Metanoiam Meriotea.
For the master of the masks is the master's mask.
Meriotea Metanoiam Maionatem Metanoiam Meriotea.
Your beloved mate, your beloved mask.

John flung the mask in light, life and water.
He saw our Lady, eternal and true.
He saw the light of the Fullness, to the mount, to the blood in the chest.
He saw the dancing masks unite.
He saw the dancing existence unite.
For the dancing masks were carried by dance.

Yes, the dancing masks were carried by dance.
The dancing masks were carried by dance.

Introduction to The Book of Adamas

The Book of Adamas is twofold; one part revealed, the other concealed. The translation of the written book, presented here, is the collection of 22 revelatory tokens, sigils or characters. The concealed, or unwritten book, is the oral transmission that accompanies it. In the Sethian tradition they are used for dreamwork, divination, and a certain practice that is difficult to describe with words. The written 'characters' were once a closely guarded secret, but since their printed exposure in 1539, they have resurfaced from time to time in a certain chain of esoteric works, mainly in France, Italy and Germany. They have flowed like a subterranean stream through several currents of the western traditions, sometimes permutating into new forms and names, but always changing that which they seep into. They have a tendency to captivate the minds and imagination of those who find them, by their enigmatic and evocative power.

The Book of Adamas

"Adamas asked for a son, so that his offspring might father the incorruptible race. Our Mother opened herself for him, and shed her blood into his dream. And through his son, the silence and the voice appeared. When this came to pass, through him, that which was dead rose itself and dissolved. This is the Book of Adamas: the twenty two drops of blood that the Mother shed into his dream, so that Seth might restore and destroy that which is, and is not. Those who draw them, grasp them and dream them will find the unwritten keys to open themselves: They are mirrors, not of the soul, but of the spirit."

AION

Boundless Nature
cannot descend
And when it does
will rise again

BEÏN

I am the Light
shining in the Darkness:
And the Darkness
Shines in the Vessel
As Silence comprehendeth me
not

GOMOR

I am the Self-Begotten:
untouched, undying
Unfolding the
Vastness
of my Being

DİN

I am the Absolute:
Unrelenting Truth
unconditional Being
continual Movement
and unbridled Beauty

HELI

The Unknown Master
makes masks
from Mirrors
Thinks Truth
from Tales
weaves Worlds
from words

VR

Two paths:
chose none.
Lightning and Truth
cannot be resisted
when they strike

ZOTH

The Dead God
sleeps in the husk of his body

The Living God
moves through the universe
in the Vessel of his Mystery

CHAMOTH

Equilibrium is not
a frozen state
but indifferent movement
between extremities

THELI

The Light-Seed coils
in the spine of the word,
under the cloak of matter,
springs forth
from silence
into ecstasy

IA

Man is a riddle whose answer is Truth
Dare to Ask
Will to Seek
Know to Knock
And keep Silent
of what is opened unto you

CATH

Art
is Desire
directed
by Will

LUZ

Sacrifice
is forsaking
what you love
and those
who love you

MOR

When the Beginning
consumes
the End,
the Instant
becomes perpetual death
and infinite resurrection

NAÏN

There are two waters
Of Heavenly Bliss
and Infernal Frenzy
And the Waters are One

XÏRON

There is a Patcher
of patterns
and pictures
With seams and stiches
binding beings together
under layers
of lies

OYN

There is a gate
into the heights of hell
into the depths of heaven
through the mirror:
Enter

PHILON

When time turns cold
and the chains change creed:
When you break against
the unmoving point,
The All will revolve around One:
and One will attain unto None

TSÏD

When darkness mixes with light
a neither-or is born

QUON

All

Many

One

All　Many　One　None　One　Many　All

One

Many

All

RASH

If the Sleeper Awakens,
If the Vessel is broken
even death
will die

SETH

The Uncreated Light
contains the world
breaks the egg
consumes Heaven
extinguishes Hell

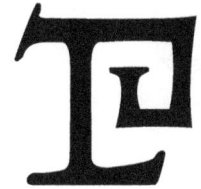

THUM

The Broken World
is a White bone Prison
a broken mirror
a cloak of smoke
a veil of words
shattering all
whom enter

Introduction to The Book of Time

The Charaxio's closing deals with the end of the world, that is, of the material world. It therefore has an eschatological character.

It is important to understand that none of the Gnostic texts can be taken literally, as it is the story behind the written word that is central; therefore, a Gnostic would never say that it is so or so because it is written here or there. This is particularly important in the reading of an apocalyptic text.

No one can know how everything will end. This will always be a subject of Pistisism (faith-based ideas), and is therefore not a central issue in the Sethian or any other Gnostic tradition.

This text is included as a natural closing of this collection, and provides a vivid image of what the ending might be like. However, there are probably just as many arguments and opinions on this subject as there are Gnostics.

You may therefore use this final book as a starting point for your own speculations on this difficult subject.

The Book of Time

The Voice of the ages whispered and sighed, "How long; for how long will this continue, for how long must we endure?
And the Great Light Eleleth turned in the infinite space and said: The time has come, Abracadabra!

The Vision in the Chapel

Eleleth once again came to the Chapel of the Four luminaries and said: The time has come for that world which is ready, and is about to turn back. You are amongst these, for you are an Aeon yourself, for you have recognized me in my two angels who came to earth. You have seen those who believe in nothing, but who hope for everything. My angels are with you, my friend.

Then I turned around, and the Gates of nature opened before me, and I saw the world and its people in their orbits. And I asked Eleleth to tell me about the end of time; the fate of mankind, and the world.
A sound as of a multitude of wings filled the place I was in, and Angels, Archangels, Principalities, Rulers, Cherubs and Seraphs approached our place from above. The sound of a mighty earthquake came from the underworld, as the Demons made place for them to hear what was said from the hills that they inhabited. For all of them wanted to hear, so they would understand, and not be destroyed on the inside of the Gate of Time.

Eleleth smiled and showed me the three human types, and said:
From the beginning there have been three forces in the world: The self-righteous, the dark daughter of the earth, and the one that is fulfilled in the world of limitations.

SETH SPEAKS

From the Fullness I heard the mighty voice of the divine and heavenly Seth; and our Father said:
Nobody is perfect in the flesh. All people are stained with innocent as well as tainted blood. No one can accomplish the law of the creator; the law is not for Man to fulfill.
Do therefore not fulfill it.
Search for me in you, search the centre that rests everywhere, but search above all for Barbelo at the delta of the Light-Water, and you shall not go astray in the world and no one shall move you, even though you move the entire creation.
Do not seek perfection in the world, for it is not there to be found.
Do not seek meaning in the world for it will give you a meaningless meaning.
Seek the company of the True Man in everyone you meet, and love them as you love the Fullness in yourself.
For your sake I will also come, and I will throw fire upon the world, in order to rob you of everything you own.
Yes, even your life will I take from you, when the Angel of Death comes into your chamber. Yes, I will come and give you of my love, the love that dissolves worlds without dissolving the Man of Light, for if you are ready to leave it all at that hour, and let everything go, you will see that you have always been ready to do this.
Then I will not have to send my creatures out to raid you; then

you are already free and can own without being owned and seek without tension. Fortify your determination, set a course that nothing in the world can interfere with, but woe to the one who lets himself go, for he will be devoured by the mouth of the greedy lion.

I am the only center of all existence and the True Being of Man, and I shall seek out those who try to keep anything back, for those who do not know me, know only death. Then through the healing poison of the snake, I will be sure that you find me, and that you thus find the Fullness. For my love is not restricted to you, but extends to all my brothers, sons and daughters. They will share in the eternal light, for I am also in them.

In your earthly form, you are like my beloved Horaia in the world, as Sofia in the darkness and Lucifer that fell burning through the darkness of a winter night.

Cain and Abel

I looked at Eleleth and he showed me a darkness and a light, and said that this is the place of Cain and Abel.

He said: The Light cannot perish. Do not believe those who say that a person is lost, for they have listened to the god of fear and foolishness. The Light cannot be lost; it can only be recognized or unrecognized. Remember that the blind see as little in the darkness of the midnight hour, as when the dawn sheds its red rays on the forests and plains of the creation.

In that respect are Cain and Abel truly brothers, for they did not know anything about the truth, if it were not for the Sons and Daughters of God, who chose them and opened their gates.

In our eyes there is no difference between those that the world has labeled sinners and those who are hailed as saints. Let the dead judge the dead and let them honor each other in their emptiness. This is the force of polarity, and the force of death through which the created world operates.

Our generation carries Light and Darkness through the world and our actions are labeled by the ignorant as good and evil and enigmatic, but know that it is only the knowledge of the Light that separates us from them.

We will reveal this knowledge to them, we will walk past them; and in our movement, we will take their precious drunkenness from them.

Since the creation of man on earth, the daughters of Cain have loved the sons of Abel; and the sons and daughters of Seth have taken their wives and husbands from amongst them. The Light is in all people, but not everyone acknowledges its existence.

Woe to the man who cannot find the truth, for he will never know true and lasting happiness. For these people all gifts and all progress will be like writing in the sand, in their endless desire for earthly achievements and fulfillment of their volatile ambitions. In the hour of death, they will fear the empty darkness.

The vision of the wandering of the Children of Seth

I then saw how our lineage was coiled through light and darkness to the underlying harmony. I saw the souls walking in a circle between the flesh and the Gates of time.
I saw how our lineage moved outside and beyond them all, and how they laid their cloaks around those straying souls, and led them through.
I also saw those who were touched by us, and thus ceased to be souls and turned into pure Light, and as such took new forms or floated into the Fullness.
I then asked Eleleth about what I saw. Why are not all the souls dissolved so that they may enter into the Fullness?

Eleleth put his arm around my soul and said: Blessed are you who are seeking the resolution and the perfect unity with the Origin; know that your being may be in pure existence if you are in perfect harmony with the Aeons of the Fullness. The souls that we dissolve are those who are unable to release their own Light. They are the ones who will not, or cannot, recognize the Fullness. In the world of matter they live meaningless lives, but Yaldabout cannot prevent people from dying the carnal death, and thus are these unfortunate creatures liberated from their journey at the end of their time.
It was these souls that Seth alluded to, when he said that he would throw a fire upon the world and watch it until everything was on fire. These fallen lights might come to peace through the descent of Seth, as Aberamento or Jesus Christ. For he has prepared an Aeon for the lost ones. It is a place, a Heaven, which may be their dwelling place, in union with his spirit. A body, which he has

called The House of his Father.

Those who enter into the Fullness as individual souls, and those who enter as part of the Body of Christ, experience the apocalypse.

THE REDEMPTION OF ALL?

Will all the generations be redeemed, I asked?
And Eleleth said: In the fullness of time all Light will once again know the Fullness. The only difference in experience is whether one is a being, or is part of the undifferentiated being. That is: whether one is an Aeon or is taking part of Aberamento's Aeon.
For all will be united in one existence without end. This is the way it is for those who know themselves and who see with the eyes of eternity.
I then recognized the need for redemption in all living things. I felt the suffering of the creation, though only temporarily, a disorder that infects people with despair, and that draws them in all directions, in search of the redemptive medicine.

The Commandments of Eleleth

Eleleth said: The way of descent is the way of ascent.

I have shown you the seals, and Seth has taught us about the sacraments, and Zorakatora has ordained.

He then said: Raise them up and open the Gates of Heaven, fly through light and darkness to the boundless limit of the Fullness, do not turn back. Throw a burning torch into the world as you depart; for I will not leave before this work is fulfilled.

When mankind finally leaves the world, the Aeons of Yaldabout and Nebroel will cease to exist. Their fate is bound to the existence of the humanity in the world. This is a great mystery that will unfold for those who know themselves.

Remember that the angels and demons of the Rulers will serve those who are of our kind. Only by uniting themselves with the Man of Light in a being that possesses Gnosis may they once again take part in the Fullness. This may be at the time when the Great Invisible Spirit withdraws the Aeon, through the fire in the thirteenth, to the Silence behind the All.

Closing words

Tetelestai!
Such is the end of the world, and thus the mystery of the dissolution for each and every man and woman to unveil.
I have revealed to you the dissolution and the end of the world. Take heed to this secret and use it with wisdom and merciless love in your encounters with the souls of humanity. Reveal and conceal, but always to the benefit of Man.

Blessed is he who knows, for he shall receive; in heaven as well as on earth. Amen!

Afterword

In this book, I have collected some of the texts that are part of the Charaxio. I have written some introductory comments on each of the books, but have avoided piercing deeply into the matter, as I think you can benefit the most if you are not told what they are really about.

With this I hope that the traditional voice has spoken clearly to those who have given it an ear, and that this book has been found to be a Gate for those who have acquired the Key.

Appendix
A self presentation of Sodalitas Sanctum Seth

Sethian Gnosticism, also called Classical Gnosticism and Sethianism, is named after Adam's third son Seth and the divine Seth, and had its 'golden age' from about 300BC to 300AD.

The Sethian tradition is probably the oldest of the Gnostic schools with common sacraments, a basic systematical theology, and a core Mystery in which the Sethians were inducted.

During the first period of about 600 years, our tradition had three major reforms as reflected in the texts that were found buried at Nag Hammadi in Egypt.
This collection of texts, the most important discovery of Gnostic literature, was probably buried since these writings were forbidden by canonical Christianity. It was found by a shepherd who initiated the challenging journey of these scriptures, before most of them were handed over to academic scholars who translated and published them.
The three Sethian periods, or reforms, were the Jewish period, the Christian period and the Platonic period. In all these reforms, the same core Gnosis or Mystery was clothed with new garments. For the vessel will always be flexible and shaped to fit the mentality and needs of the present time.

The hallmark of Gnosticism is its systematic enquiring approach to redemption; it is a methodical approach to salvation.

This tradition is based on a homo-centric reading of the Biblical stories of creation, the nature of God, how humanity came to live on earth, and how we may recapture an enlightened fullness of being. Critical reading of the acts and intentions of the Creator as described in the Bible gives Gnostics reason to suspect that this entity is far from being a God who loves humankind, and who seeks its fulfillment and peace. Rather than participating in a lowly spiritual and mental warfare that will last as long as there are people cherishing this myth, Gnostics seek the Pleroma and The Great Invisible Spirit; concepts of a fullness that transcends all worldly and mental structures.

Sethianism thus relies on personal experience and scientific understanding of humanity and religion, rather than fate.

The Sethian scriptures are important tools; initiatory journeys written to enlighten us and make way for the grand eureka that will turn our eyes from the shadows on the wall, to the light behind us.

Sethianism is thus not a religious path as such, but rather a path between the paths. It perpetuates a story told at the strike of the thirteenth hour on the mystical dial of the wise; from a mental position between truth and falsehood, reality and dream, at a spiritual crossroad in a point without a centre.

Sodalitas Sanctum Seth (SSS) is a modern heir to the Sethian tradition, yet even though the SSS is a modern manifestation, it perpetuates the same Mystery as that of the Sethian schools of old.
The scriptures, sacraments, and rituals of the SSS are collected in a book called Charaxio, to commemorate the mountain where

Seth had hid his teachings until the time was reap for the Sethian initiators, to once again walk the earth.

The founding master of the SSS was also given an Ethiopian Gnostic succession that predates the so-called Gnostic revival of the 1880's. The story of this legacy is not yet to be revealed to the public, due to the wishes of the previous master. This transmission is however used to yet again light the Sethian beacon at the edge of reality.

The Sodalitas Sanctum Seth consists of the following houses that are to be revealed to the world at the present time. Membership in one or all of the houses is by invitation only.

The Fellowship of the Serpent and the Dove - The Fellowship is the fellowship of seekers, who seek to approach Sethian Gnosis. This is the house of the lay Sethians, who work with minimal guidance from the Convent, on an individual basis.

The Circle - The Circle is the sanctuary of men and women who work towards individual accomplishment; in a master and apprentice relationship. This is the 'Sethian School'.

The Convent - The Convent is the sanctuary of the masters. This is the only house that utilizes the name: Sodalitas Sanctum Seth.

The following English writings on the Sodalitas Sanctum Seth have been approved by our organization:

Ødegaard, Rune: *The Gate: Sethian Gnosticism in the postmodern world*. 2012 Krystiania publishing, Oslo Norway

Ødegaard, Rune: *The Key: Sethian Gnosticism in the postmodern world*. 2011 Krystiania publishing, Oslo Norway

The homepage of the SSS: www.charaxio.org

JI: Does anyone else know about this?

JC: No, and this is how I want it to remain.

JI: Do you really understand what you ask of me?

JC: Yes, but it is our only option, if we shall be able to make clear to the others what we have discovered. They need to experience it for themselves; and we can give them that.

JI: I know, but do you think they will be able to live with the truth?

JC: I hope so ... You must go now.

JI: See you tonight.

JC: Good luck, see you when all of this is over.

JI: Yeah, good luck. In a few days it will be all over ....

www.ingramcontent.com/pod-product-compliance
Lightning Source LLC
Chambersburg PA
CBHW030400100426
42812CB00028B/2777/J